BIBLE WARS & WEAPONS

WITHDRAWN

Other *2:52 Soul Gear* Books

Non-fiction
Bible Heroes & Bad Guys
Weird & Gross Bible Stuff
Bible Fortresses, Temples & Tombs

Fiction
Laptop 1/Reality Shift
Laptop 2/Double Take
Laptop 3/Explosive Secrets
Laptop 4/Power Play

smarter · stronger

2:52

deeper · cooler

BIBLEWARS
&WEAPONS

WRITTEN BY
RICK**OSBORNE**
MARNIE**WOODING**
ED**STRAUSS**

ILLUSTRATED BY
MICHAEL**MOORE**

Zonder**kidz**

Zonder**kidz**™
The children's group of Zondervan

www.zonderkidz.com

Bible Wars & Weapons
Copyright © 2002 by Rick Osborne
Illustrations Copyright © 2002 by Michael Moore

Requests for information should be addressed to:
Grand Rapids, Michigan 49530

ISBN: 0-310-70323-9

Acquisitions Editor: Gwen Ellis
Project Editor: Pat Matuszak
Art direction and design: Michelle Lenger

Printed in United States
02 03 04 05/RRD/5 4 3 2 1

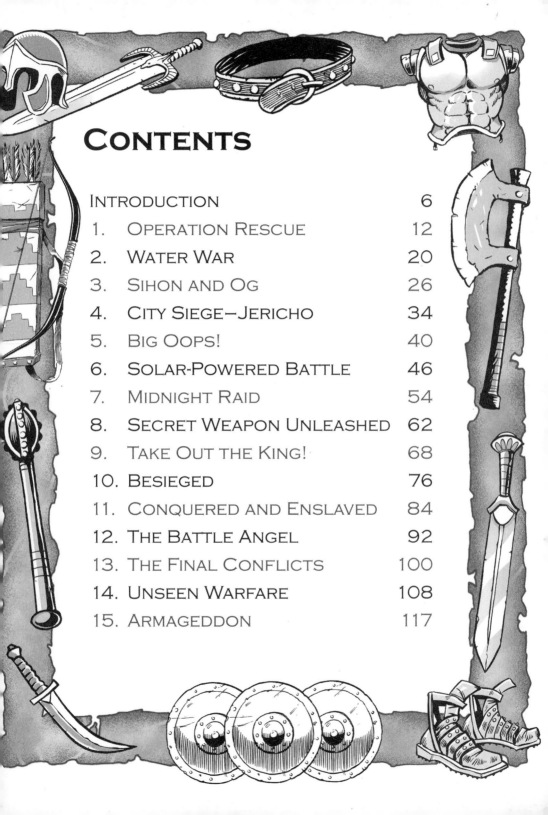

CONTENTS

INTRODUCTION

If you think the Bible is a big snooze full of
boring people sitting around talking about
the best way to be holy, oh man—you are
not even warm. The Bible has more action
than a big Hollywood action movie, more
sword clashing, fortress smashing, and
hand-to-hand combat than a video game,
and more gross, disgusting, eyeball-popping
weirdness than a special effects department.
The Bible is full of amazing, godly warriors
who battled against outrageous odds to
defend God's people. If you think soldiers are
tough now–ho!–wait till you check out these
ancient iron men.

The Bible has it all: unstoppable generals,
armies so large no way you could count the
soldiers–fortresses under attack–even armies of
angels in chariots and fire shooting down from the
sky. There are wars where hail, thunder, floods, and
earthquakes were all part of the battle plan. Yup, the
Bible gives the inside story on the most miraculous,
spectacular warfare ever seen in the history of the
world.

There's more: There was another invisible, terrible,
bone-shaking battle waged behind the scenes–part of

the one big war to rescue the world from slavery to sin and death. In the spirit world, Satan constantly planned military strategies for his army of demons to control the world, but God was always WAY ahead of him. Time and again, the Lord kick-boxed Satan into a corner and led God's people to victory. Want the details? Then come explore the world of sword-slicing, shield-shattering, blood-splattered Bible battles! Keep your helmet strapped on and your head attached to your shoulders, and you will see.

WHERE IN THE WORLD DID THE BIBLE BATTLES HAPPEN?

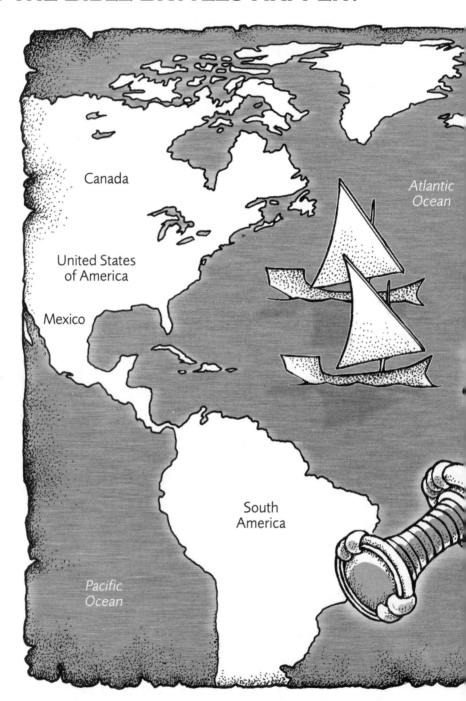

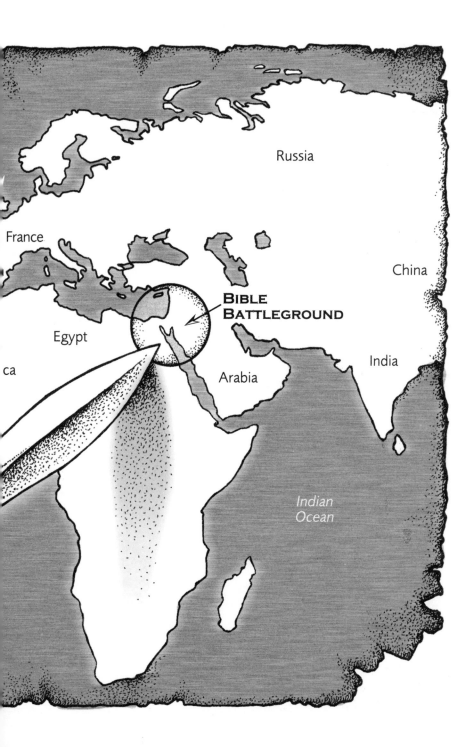

Russia

France

China

**BIBLE
BATTLEGROUND**

Egypt

India

ca

Arabia

*Indian
Ocean*

WEIRD STUFF:
WEAPONS OF THE BIBLE

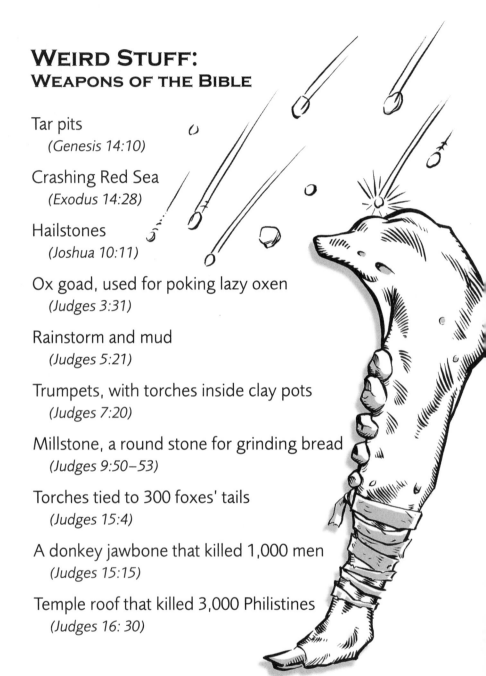

Tar pits
  (Genesis 14:10)

Crashing Red Sea
  (Exodus 14:28)

Hailstones
  (Joshua 10:11)

Ox goad, used for poking lazy oxen
  (Judges 3:31)

Rainstorm and mud
  (Judges 5:21)

Trumpets, with torches inside clay pots
  (Judges 7:20)

Millstone, a round stone for grinding bread
  (Judges 9:50–53)

Torches tied to 300 foxes' tails
  (Judges 15:4)

A donkey jawbone that killed 1,000 men
  (Judges 15:15)

Temple roof that killed 3,000 Philistines
  (Judges 16: 30)

MAP
LEGEND

     ARMY'S AND
ARMY CAMPS

ARMY PATHS

    BATTLE ZONES

LAND

SEIGE OF A CITY

OPERATION RESCUE
[GENESIS 14]

Who:
Abraham and his allies vs. the Kings of the Northern Alliance

Where:
The mountains, valleys, and plains of Canaan—Dan to Hobah

Weapons:
Hot pursuit, swords, and screams

Abram (who was later renamed Abraham, by God) lived in the central mountains of Canaan (Israel) and his nephew, Lot, lived in the city of Sodom, in the southern part of Canaan. There had been some angry words between the two men's herders, and so they decided to go separate ways. Abram let Lot choose

which part of the land he wanted. Lot chose the cities
of the well-watered plains, and that was his first mis-
take. You see, most of the violent wars happened in
the cities of the plains. No one bothered Abram, up in
the mountains.

Well, one day Abram was just watching his sheep and
talking to God when a man staggered into his camp
gasping that invading kings had carried off loot and

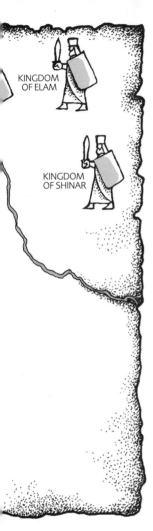

people from Sodom and nearby Gomorrah. Lot lived in Sodom and he was one of the prisoners taken away! Abram was usually a pretty peaceful guy, but not this time. He was going to rescue Lot.

BATTLE MAP:
Battle in the Valley of Siddim

Invading Kingdoms from the North:

- Elam
- Shinar
- Ellasar
- Goiim

Defeated Tribes and Territories:

- Rephaites in *Ashteroth Karnaim*
- Zuzites in *Ham*
- Emites in *Shaveh Kiriathaim*
- Horites in *Seir*
- Amalekites in *En Mishpat*
- Amorites of *Hazazon Tamar*

Defeated Cities in the South:

- Gomorrah
- Admah
- Zeboiim
- Zoar
- Sodom

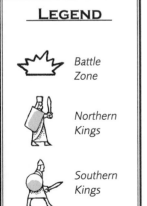

LEGEND

Battle Zone

Northern Kings

Southern Kings

The trouble had started when King Kedor-laomer and three other northern kings formed an alliance and invaded cities in Canaan. They thought it looked pretty easy to spend a couple of months fighting and collecting loot—horses, sheep, treasure, food, and slaves—and then go home. So this northern alliance worked its way south by first attacking cities in Ashteroth Karnaim, Ham, Shaveh Kiriathaim, the hills of Seir, En Mishpat, and Hazazon Tamar.

That done, they were ready for dessert! The five biggest, ripest, wealthiest cities were just sitting there for the taking. These were:

- Gomorrah
- Admah
- Zeboiim
- Zoar
- Sodom

The five kings of these big southern cities formed an alliance of their own and got together in the Valley of Siddim. They freaked out when they saw the armies of the northern alliance marching on them. Time for a huddle. They pulled their armies together to defend their turf. They thought they had the home-field advantage. But they were wrong. Four battle-hardened, huge, nasty, head-smashing northern armies were marching against five terrified, weak armies more used to soft living than to battle.

The five southern kings bravely went to war, but when they got a good look at the armies of the northern alliance, they took to the hills, leaving their cities unprotected. Not very kingly, would you say?

The northern alliance armies swept into the cities and took everything worth anything. Then they headed home. One of their pieces of loot was Abram's nephew, Lot. They also took many other people as slaves.

No sooner had the messenger finished telling his story than Abram immediately got together his 318 trained men and called on his Amorite neighbors to join him. Abram was going to track down those thieving Amorites and get his family back, or die trying. Here's what happened.

BATTLE MAP:
Rescue Mission

This map shows the rescue mission and attack on the caravan of the Northern kings by Abram. Features: Mamre, Dan, Hobah, and Valley of Shaveh.

Abram and his allies set out in hot pursuit of the northern army. They caught up quickly because the invaders' caravan was loaded down with plunder,

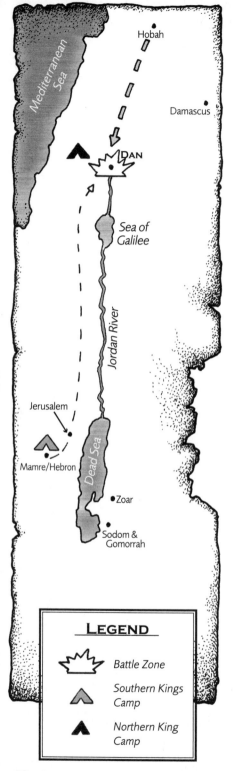

Hobah

Mediterranean Sea

Damascus

DAN

Sea of Galilee

Jordan River

Jerusalem

Mamre/Hebron

Dead Sea

Zoar

Sodom & Gomorrah

LEGEND

Battle Zone

Southern Kings Camp

Northern King Camp

slaves, and herds and was moving slowly.

The northern alliance set up camp near the city of Dan. An angry Abram watched them from the hills. When the enemy was all bedded down and asleep, Abraham split up his men into groups and attacked.

At Abram's signal, his fighters rushed out of the darkness, screaming war cries and lopping off heads. The great northern army was terrified and scrambling out of their beds they for their lives. Abram chased them as far as the hills north of Damascus.

Abram found Lot among the prisoners and rescued him and all the people and all the treasures that had been looted from the cities.

Lot was one very grateful nephew. He thanked his uncle and he thanked God. The battle was over and everyone went home.

GET COOLER

Sometimes other people need our help. Abram had to rescue Lot. He chased the bad guys until they dropped. Family is important and sometimes we need to help each other. Okay, okay, maybe marauding northern invaders won't nab your relatives and carry them off so that you have to rescue them. But sometimes we have to put aside our own plans to help others—like mowing your grandparents' lawn instead of going to the mall. Stuff like mowing lawns isn't overly dangerous or exciting (unless the lawn mower runs over you), but it is giving your time and energy to help others, and that's a good thing to do. It is the kind of thing a good and brave man will do—even a young man like you.

WATER WAR
[EXODUS 17:8–16]

Who:
Moses, Joshua, and the Israelites vs. the Amalekites

Where:
The hot, dry, sandy Sinai Desert

Weapons:
Strong arms, maces, long spears, bows and arrows, daggers, and armor

This story puts a whole new spin on water fights! Abraham was dead, and his son Isaac, his grandson Jacob, and Jacob's twelve sons were long gone too. The descendents of Jacob became known as Israelites, because God gave Jacob the name Israel. The Israelites had become slaves in Egypt. Moses led them out of Egypt, and they were on the way back to Canaan—God had promised Abraham, Isaac, and Jacob that Canaan would be their homeland. The Israelites traveled through the scorching, scorpion-filled, sandy Sinai Desert. This place was grim. There was not even one corner convenience store where you could stop and buy a slushy. Finding an oasis with enough water for two or three million people–plus animals–was tough business. And now for the BAD news: godless desert nomads called Amalekites claimed all this waterless land as their turf. Yeah, even though it had no water.

The Israelites camped in a bone-dry, dusty valley at a place called Rephidim. Of course, they were complaining and moaning about the lack of water. Solution? God pointed out a rock and told Moses, "Hit it with your staff." Moses obeyed, and water instantly gushed out! Enough water for all two or three million Israelites!

Remember, there had never been water there before. When news of this new watering hole got out, the Amalekites' eyes bugged out with greed. Hey! This is OUR land! That makes this new oasis OUR oasis. (Never mind that GOD gave this water to the Israelites. The Amalekites probably thought that the Israelites had just dug a well in their land.)

The Amalekites worked themselves into a war frenzy. Look! Millions of strangers are slurping up our water! We gotta stop them before they drink the well dry! Howling like a pack of hyenas, the Amalekites attacked.

Mediterranean Sea

Dead Sea

Goshen

Elim

Red Sea

REPHIDIM

LEGEND

Battle Zone

Amalekite Land

Exodus of Moses, Joshua & Israelites

Israelite Camp

BATTLE MAP:
Water War

So Moses chose a warrior named Joshua to command the Israelite forces. Scramble! Scramble! Red Alert! Violent warfare erupted on the battlefield. Moses stood on a hill overlooking the battlefield with his staff held high over his head. As long as Moses' hands were high, the Israelites were winning. But when he dropped his hands they started to lose. Well, prop that guy up!

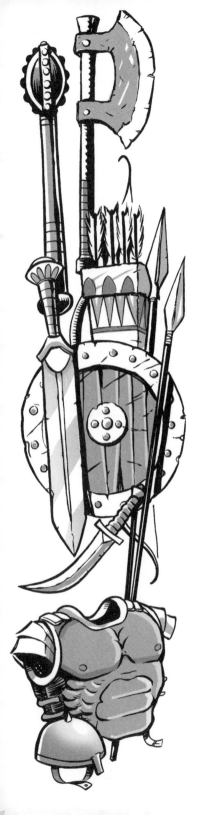

Two other people helped hold Moses' arms up when he got tired. (You try holding your arms above your head for just ten minutes.) In the end, the Israelites whipped those Amalekites hands down—ummm—make that hands up.

What type of army did Joshua have? Not a very well-armed or well-trained army, that's for sure. The Israelites had rock-hard muscles—they had done hard labor all their lives—but they had little training as fighters. Maybe Joshua found some skilled soldiers who had fought in the Egyptian army and still had some of their gear. They might have had maces (heavy balls on chains), long spears, bows, bronze-tipped arrows, bronze daggers, axes, swords, shields, and body armor.

But most of Joshua's recruits had been stone-chiseling, mud-pit-stomping, brick-making slaves and didn't have proper weapons. So—were they doomed? Nah. They had God on their side. Hey, better a bad weapon with God's help than a great weapon without him.

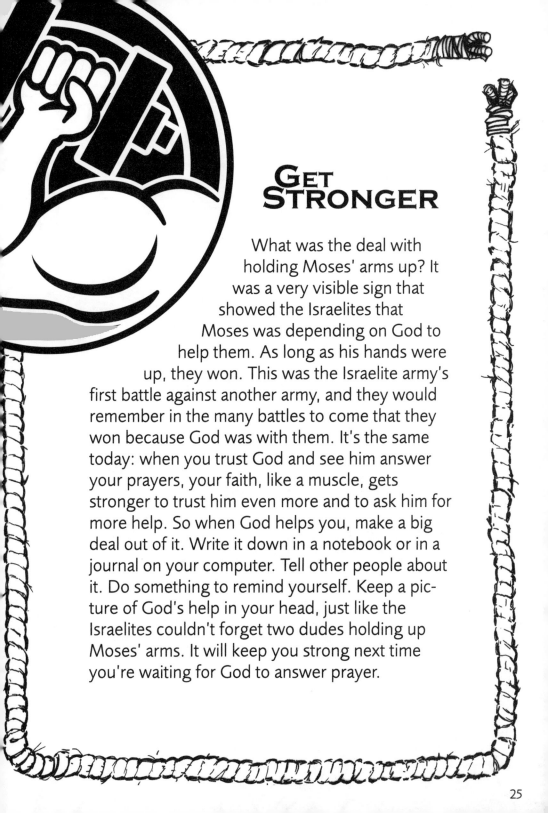

GET STRONGER

What was the deal with holding Moses' arms up? It was a very visible sign that showed the Israelites that Moses was depending on God to help them. As long as his hands were up, they won. This was the Israelite army's first battle against another army, and they would remember in the many battles to come that they won because God was with them. It's the same today: when you trust God and see him answer your prayers, your faith, like a muscle, gets stronger to trust him even more and to ask him for more help. So when God helps you, make a big deal out of it. Write it down in a notebook or in a journal on your computer. Tell other people about it. Do something to remind yourself. Keep a picture of God's help in your head, just like the Israelites couldn't forget two dudes holding up Moses' arms. It will keep you strong next time you're waiting for God to answer prayer.

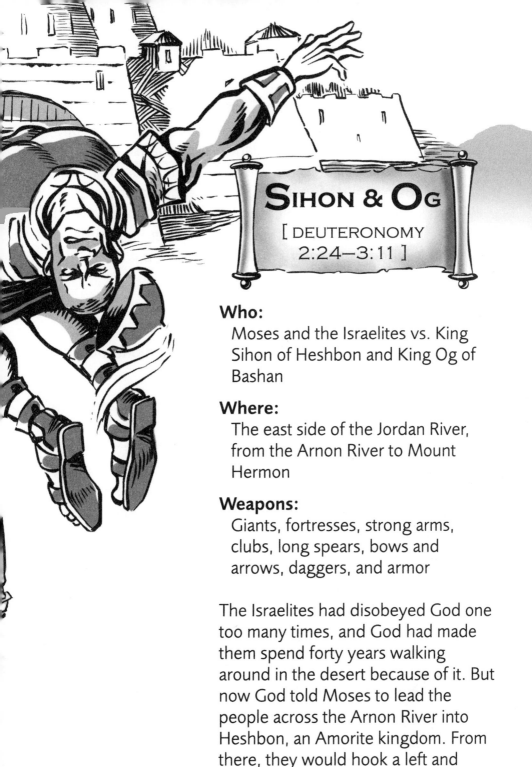

SIHON & OG

[DEUTERONOMY
2:24–3:11]

Who:
Moses and the Israelites vs. King Sihon of Heshbon and King Og of Bashan

Where:
The east side of the Jordan River, from the Arnon River to Mount Hermon

Weapons:
Giants, fortresses, strong arms, clubs, long spears, bows and arrows, daggers, and armor

The Israelites had disobeyed God one too many times, and God had made them spend forty years walking around in the desert because of it. But now God told Moses to lead the people across the Arnon River into Heshbon, an Amorite kingdom. From there, they would hook a left and cross the Jordan River into Canaan, at last. Moses sent messages to Sihon, king of Heshbon, saying, "Hey, man, can we travel through your land? We promise that all two or three million of us will stay on the main highway. We'll pay in silver for any food we eat or water we drink. You stand to earn some cash here, dude." Sihon said no. The Israelites scratched their heads. Other kingdoms had let them pass through. What was the big deal?

BATTLE MAP:
Israel vs. Sihon and Og

Sihon got his troops together and marched out to fight the Israelites at a place called Jahaz.

Joshua rolled his eyes. OK, if this is how you want it. He sent out a fighting force that had grown tough through training and forty years of desert living and fighting. With God's help, they whipped Sihon and took over the whole kingdom of Heshbon. Oh yeah—they destroyed his cities and killed everybody in them. Talk about a tough lesson in sharing!

Then the Israelites attacked Bashan, where the giant, a big guy named Og, reigned supreme. Og was one of the last of an ancient tribe who were unusually tall. So he figured he was big enough to fight puny Israelites, even if they'd beaten Sihon. King Og's land wasn't even on the Israelites' "to-conquer" list.But Og didn't like these new guys so he sent his army south to stop them.

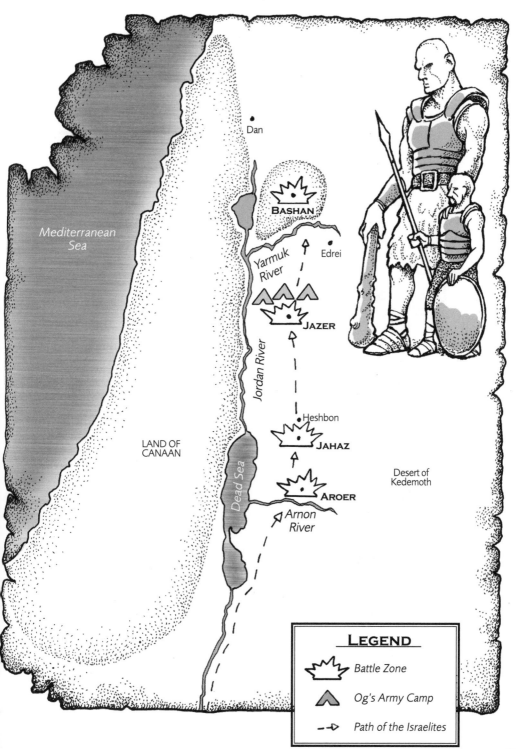

Dan

BASHAN

Mediterranean
Sea

Edrei

Yarmuk
River

JAZER

Jordan River

LAND OF
CANAAN

Heshbon

JAHAZ

Dead Sea

AROER

Desert of
Kedemoth

Arnon
River

LEGEND

Battle Zone

Og's Army Camp

--> Path of the Israelites

Og really made the Israelites nervous–in fact, downright scared? But God told them NOT to worry because Big Og was going for a hard fall! God helped the Israelites. The armies clashed, in a big way! When the dust settled, Og was just another oversized casualty, and the Israelites had bashed Bashan, leaving no survivors. Well, except for the cattle. Joshua and his swat team then swept through the land destroying all 60 walled cities and a bunch of unwalled villages.

Moses handed Sihon's territory over to the family of Jacob's son Gad. He gave Og's land to the family of Jacob's grandson Manasseh.

The Israelites would have paid Heshbon a fortune in silver for their quiet little stopover in his kingdom. Hey, it's not like they would've sucked his wells dry. And Bashan? They had no plans to attack Bashan. Both Og

and Sihon ended up in the history book of dumb battle moves by ignoring peaceful solutions. Nope, it's nooot smart to put out roadblocks when God's on the move.

Big Guy–Short World

King Og was a big and important guy. Big, because—he was big. His iron bed was a whopping 13 feet long and 6 feet wide. It was also impressive because iron was a new thing in Canaan. After Og was gone, his bed was kept on display, as kind of an ancient tourist stop. Hey, even back then people were curious! Og was the last of the giant Rephaites.

GET COOLER

Sometimes, no matter
what good and kind
things you do, there will
be people, who–for whatever
reason–will not like you. They will
talk against you. What to do? Try everything you can to work things out, but if they
don't give an inch, and you know that you're
doing what God told us to do–to love our
enemies. Just keep on going. Don't let critics
get you down or stand in your way. Be as
kind as you can to them and pray for them,
but keep going. Don't let Og-sized roadblocks stop you from following God.

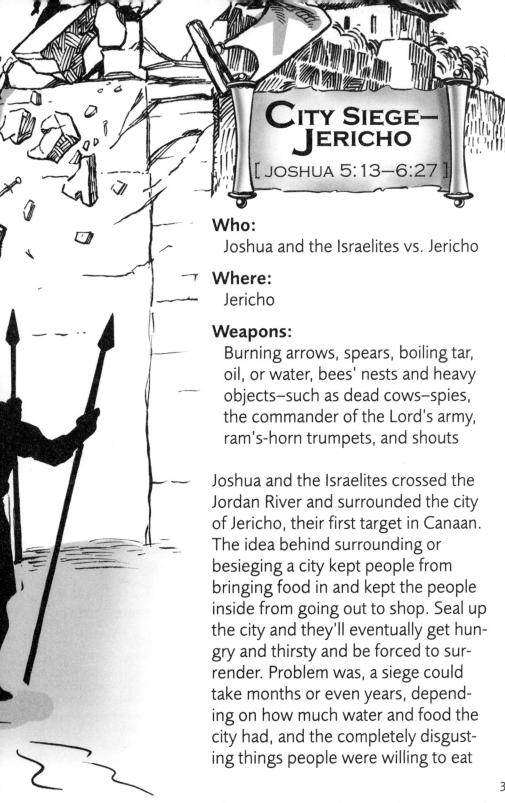

CITY SIEGE— JERICHO

[JOSHUA 5:13–6:27]

Who:
Joshua and the Israelites vs. Jericho

Where:
Jericho

Weapons:
Burning arrows, spears, boiling tar, oil, or water, bees' nests and heavy objects–such as dead cows–spies, the commander of the Lord's army, ram's-horn trumpets, and shouts

Joshua and the Israelites crossed the Jordan River and surrounded the city of Jericho, their first target in Canaan. The idea behind surrounding or besieging a city kept people from bringing food in and kept the people inside from going out to shop. Seal up the city and they'll eventually get hungry and thirsty and be forced to surrender. Problem was, a siege could take months or even years, depending on how much water and food the city had, and the completely disgusting things people were willing to eat when food ran out. If a city held out long enough, the besieging army might get distracted with another battle or move on to an easier target. But this didn't happen at Jericho.

BATTLE MAP:
The Walls of Jericho

The people of Jericho were scared right down to the bone by the Israelites. They had watched for months as the Israelites took over the cities of Heshbon and Bashan. Jericho stockpiled water and food, preparing for a looong siege. The city had high, super–thick stone walls, and its people hoped the Israelites would give up on the siege thing and go after some easier targets instead.

Why siege Jericho, anyway? Why didn't the Israelites just attack? Well– fighting from below while your enemy is high above

JERICHO

Jordan River

Dead Sea

This is one way to enter a city, however, this was not the way Jericho was conquered.

is a problem. First you have to find a way to break down the gates or dig under or climb the walls. While you're doing all this breaking and digging and climbing, your enemy is having fun dropping bricks, boulders, boiling oil, hornets' nests, and even rotten, dead cows on top of you—or shooting arrows into you. Not fun for you, of course.

When God told Joshua that he had a plan to take Jericho, Joshua was all ears. Next thing you know, the Israelites were quietly marching around the city (out of arrow range, to be sure). Not a solider whispered a word. They did this once a day for six days. Can you imagine how this puzzled and terrified Jericho's people? On the seventh day, however, Joshua's marchers went around the city seven times. Then they let loose and shouted battle cries, and the priests

wailed away on rams' horns!

Noise? That's it? Yup! That's it. Suddenly, Jericho's colossal walls collapsed and crashed to the ground with a thunderous roar and huge clouds of dust. And just like that, Joshua and his soldiers scrambled over the dusty rubble and took the city.

The Spy Guys

Before the Israelites attacked, Joshua sent spies to check out the layout and defenses of Jericho. Joshua wanted to know how strong the walls were, what kind of weapons the town had, how big its food supplies were, and how many defenders the Israelites would face.

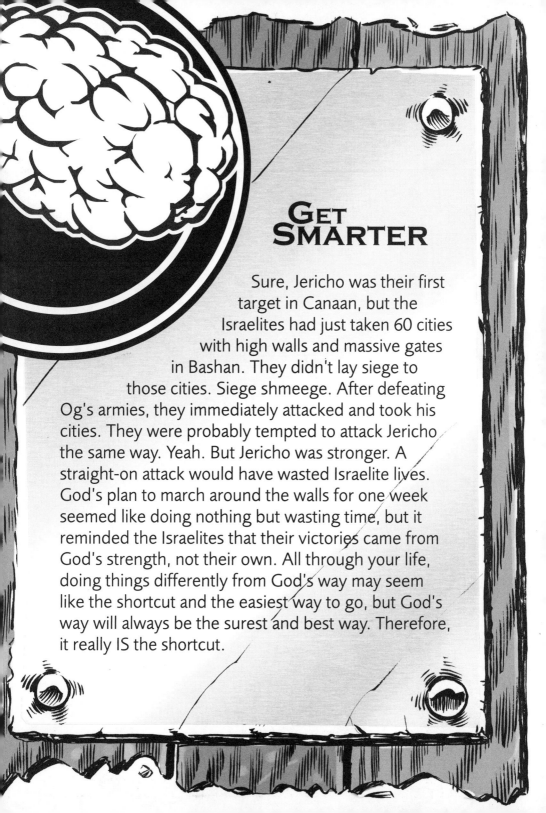

GET SMARTER

Sure, Jericho was their first target in Canaan, but the Israelites had just taken 60 cities with high walls and massive gates in Bashan. They didn't lay siege to those cities. Siege shmeege. After defeating Og's armies, they immediately attacked and took his cities. They were probably tempted to attack Jericho the same way. Yeah. But Jericho was stronger. A straight-on attack would have wasted Israelite lives. God's plan to march around the walls for one week seemed like doing nothing but wasting time, but it reminded the Israelites that their victories came from God's strength, not their own. All through your life, doing things differently from God's way may seem like the shortcut and the easiest way to go, but God's way will always be the surest and best way. Therefore, it really IS the shortcut.

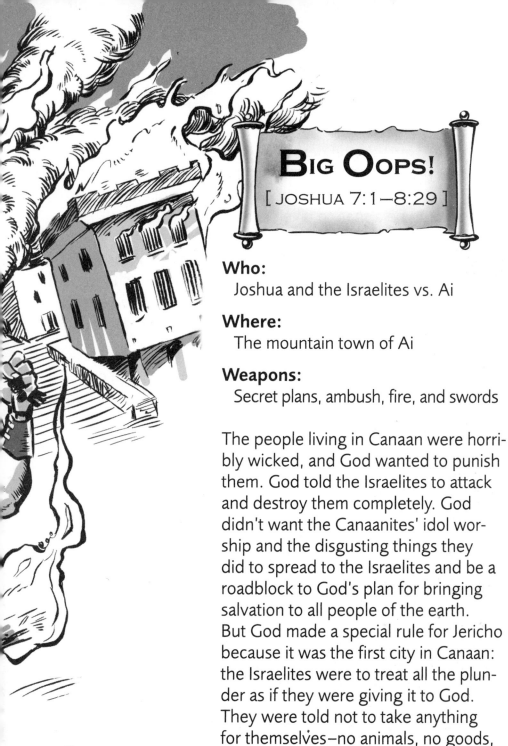

Big Oops!

[JOSHUA 7:1—8:29]

Who:
Joshua and the Israelites vs. Ai

Where:
The mountain town of Ai

Weapons:
Secret plans, ambush, fire, and swords

The people living in Canaan were horribly wicked, and God wanted to punish them. God told the Israelites to attack and destroy them completely. God didn't want the Canaanites' idol worship and the disgusting things they did to spread to the Israelites and be a roadblock to God's plan for bringing salvation to all people of the earth. But God made a special rule for Jericho because it was the first city in Canaan: the Israelites were to treat all the plunder as if they were giving it to God. They were told not to take anything for themselves—no animals, no goods, no gold, nothing.

BATTLE MAP:
The Seige at Ai

After Jericho, the next city on Joshua's list was the little hill town of Ai. Joshua again sent some spies to check out the target. The report? Piece of cake. It would be a snap to take because it had only a few troops. Joshua was so confident that he sent only 3,000 soldiers to storm the city. Surprise, surprise! Next thing you know, the guys from Ai were chasing the Israelites back down the hill! They cornered some in a rock quarry and by the end of the battle had killed 36 of them.

This stunned Joshua. Hadn't God promised him only victories? If word got out that a weak town like Ai had

whipped Israel, their tough reputation was toast. Joshua threw himself on the ground in front of the ark of the Lord and prayed.

God informed Joshua that someone had disobeyed his orders by taking things from Jericho. (Remember, Josh? The rule there was, no soldier was to snag any of the good stuff—it was God's share.) If Joshua wanted God to help his army, he had to

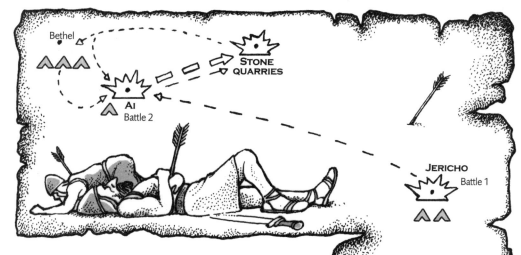

Bethel

STONE QUARRIES

Ai
Battle 2

JERICHO
Battle 1

sort it out. Finally Achan was identified as the screwup.

After he was caught redhanded, he admitted taking some way-cool clothes, a bunch of silver, and a bar of gold from Jericho. Achan and his family paid for his greed with their lives. Now Joshua went back to ask God how to take Ai.

God gave Joshua a totally cool strategy. Joshua marched 30,000 of his best fighters up to Ai. About 25,000 of them camped north of the town. The other 5,000 soldiers crept between Ai and its nearby ally, Bethel. They set an ambush. The next morning, Joshua and the 25,000 marched up toward the front gate of Ai. The king of Ai

ACHEN

JOSHUA

LEGEND

Battle Zone

Israelite Camp

Israelite Army

Ai Army

43

couldn't take his eyes off them.

At first light, chaaarrge! The king and most of his army rushed out of the city gates and attacked Joshua's main force. Joshua's soldiers pretended to run away—just like before. The Ai army, shouting victory cries, chased Joshua's army eastward toward the desert. When Joshua gave the signal, the 5,000 Israelites behind Ai jumped out of the bushes, captured the unprotected city, and set it on fire.

When the soldiers from Ai looked back and saw their city going up in smoke, they knew it was no pot roast burning. Suddenly, the fleeing Israelites stopped running and turned to fight.

The king of Ai and his army tried to run back the way they'd come, but by then the 5,000 ambushers were coming from the burning city. Trapped! Ai's army became an Ai sandwich.

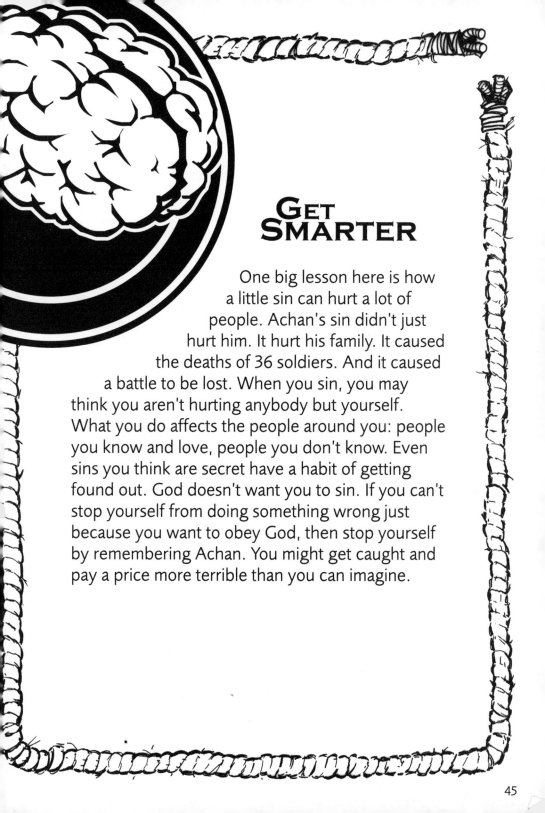

GET SMARTER

One big lesson here is how a little sin can hurt a lot of people. Achan's sin didn't just hurt him. It hurt his family. It caused the deaths of 36 soldiers. And it caused a battle to be lost. When you sin, you may think you aren't hurting anybody but yourself. What you do affects the people around you: people you know and love, people you don't know. Even sins you think are secret have a habit of getting found out. God doesn't want you to sin. If you can't stop yourself from doing something wrong just because you want to obey God, then stop yourself by remembering Achan. You might get caught and pay a price more terrible than you can imagine.

SOLAR-POWERED BATTLE
[JOSHUA 10]

Who:
The Gibeonites, Joshua, and the Israelites vs. King Adoni-Zedek of the Amorites and his Allies

Where:
Gibeon and cities north of Jerusalem

Weapons:
Treaties, tricks, swords, hailstones, prayer, and the sun

When the people from Gibeon and three of its neighbors found out God's rule for waging war in Canaan—wipe out everyone—they tried to figure out a plan to save themselves. They knew that if they didn't fight the Israelites, they would be wiped out. And if they fought the Israelites, well—they'd still get wiped out. They knew that nobody could stand up to the God of Israel. They came up with a plan that they hoped would save their lives.

BATTLE MAP: The Solar-Powered Battle

The plan was so dangerous they must have discussed it till their jaws ached. Still, it was better than plan A (being killed), and plan B (being killed). Some Gibeonites dressed in old clothes and patched, worn sandals. They led donkeys loaded down with old wineskins and moldy bread into Israelite HQ near the Jordan River. "Make a peace treaty with us," they said. "We're from a distant country." Distant? Gibeon was only 15 miles away.

LEGEND

Battle Zone

Israelite Camp

Path of the Israelites

Path of Amorite Army of Jerusalem

Jordan River

GIBEON

Kiraith Jearim

AZEKAH

Jerusalem

Gilgal

MAKKEDAH

JOSHUA'S CAMP

Eglon

Lachish

Hebron

Dead Sea

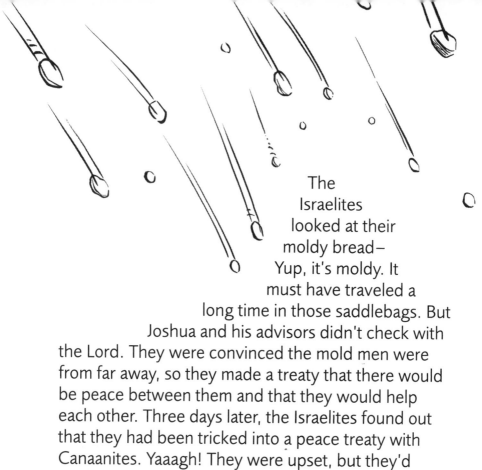

The
Israelites
looked at their
moldy bread—
Yup, it's moldy. It
must have traveled a
long time in those saddlebags. But
Joshua and his advisors didn't check with
the Lord. They were convinced the mold men were
from far away, so they made a treaty that there would
be peace between them and that they would help
each other. Three days later, the Israelites found out
that they had been tricked into a peace treaty with
Canaanites. Yaaagh! They were upset, but they'd
made a promise and couldn't break it.

When the king of Jerusalem, Adoni-Zedek, heard
about the Gibeonites' peace treaty, he got a bunch of
other Amorite kings to kindly join him in attacking the
city of Gibeon.

Joshua had to quickly muster his army to help his new
allies. An Israelite strike force marched all night and
caught the Amorites by surprise. In the early morning
light, thousands of Israelites rushed the Amorite
camps with swinging swords. The Amorites took off

running. God got into the act himself by sending helmet-denting hailstones at the bad guys.

But the Amorites were scattering, and Joshua worried that they might escape if the Israelites didn't chase them down before nightfall. Joshua asked the Lord to make the sun and the moon stand still in the sky—giving him more daylight to finish the battle. Amazingly, the sun stayed high in the sky for an entire day!

"The Lord was fighting for Israel!"

Joshua's soldiers had been awake all one day, had marched all night, had fought until the sun was high, then had fought another full day. Like, were they tired or what?

Canaan was a wild territory with many ethnic groups— tribes. Each group built or conquered its own settlements and cities. One little city against the world wasn't very strong by itself. But if that city joined forces with one or two other cities, it made all of them stronger. So villages and cities joined together for trade and support. The principle: You pick a fight with me, you've picked a fight with all my friends too!

GET COOLER

Even though the Gibeonites had tricked him, Joshua had given his word and wouldn't go back on it. If you want to be the kind of man of God Joshua was, you have to keep your word. Make this your motto: "If I say it, it's the truth. If I say it, you can count on me to do it." When you make promises to people, you, like Joshua, have to do what you say you will. God always keeps his promises and commitments. We should keep ours, too!

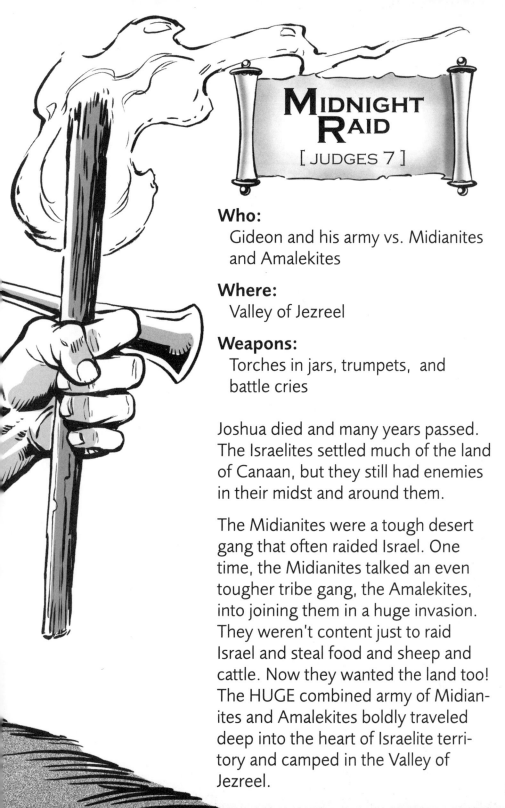

Midnight Raid
[JUDGES 7]

Who:
Gideon and his army vs. Midianites and Amalekites

Where:
Valley of Jezreel

Weapons:
Torches in jars, trumpets, and battle cries

Joshua died and many years passed. The Israelites settled much of the land of Canaan, but they still had enemies in their midst and around them.

The Midianites were a tough desert gang that often raided Israel. One time, the Midianites talked an even tougher tribe gang, the Amalekites, into joining them in a huge invasion. They weren't content just to raid Israel and steal food and sheep and cattle. Now they wanted the land too! The HUGE combined army of Midianites and Amalekites boldly traveled deep into the heart of Israelite territory and camped in the Valley of Jezreel.

BATTLE MAP:
Gideon's Midnight Raid

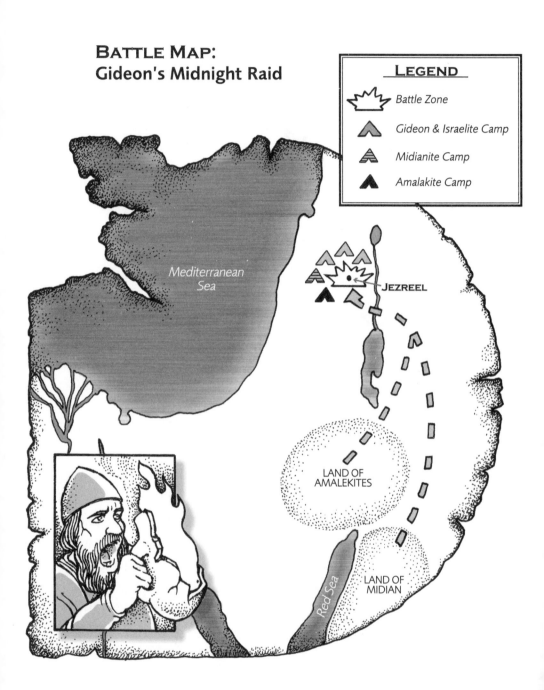

LEGEND

- Battle Zone
- Gideon & Israelite Camp
- Midianite Camp
- Amalakite Camp

Mediterranean Sea

JEZREEL

LAND OF AMALEKITES

LAND OF MIDIAN

Red Sea

God sent an angel to make a dude named Gideon the general of the Israelites who would fight the huge invasion force. Gideon gathered a big army of 32,000 fighters, but God wanted to show Gideon and all of Israel that he—God—was going to win the war for them. If the army were too big, the Israelites would high-five each other and think they had won the battle themselves. So God told Gideon to send everybody home except for a very small strike force. That made it **300** Israelites against an army of well over **135,000** Midianites and Amalekites. Ho! Some odds—450 to 1! If the Israelites won, it would be a massive, phenomenal, mammoth miracle. Well, guess what! One miracle coming up!

God gave Gideon an outrageous and daring battle plan. That night, Gideon and his commandos crept toward the enemy camp in the valley. Quietly, Gideon stationed his 300 soldiers in three companies around the enemy camp. Gideon's raiders silently assembled their strange equipment. It was the middle of the night, just after the changing of the guard. Ready, guys? Ready.

Out of the darkness, the Midianites and Amalekites were blasted awake by the sound of hundreds of war trumpets from every direction, followed by crashing, like the sound of a huge army making its way down the dark slopes above them. They leaped out of their beds in terror. Bloodcurdling battle cries were all around them. They thought a mighty Israelite army had surrounded them!

The Midianites pulled their swords and started slashing at anything and everything that came near them in the dark. "Oops, sorry, Charlie—didn't know it was you."

Gideon and his force didn't have to do a thing! They stayed safely outside the camp and watched by firelight as Midianites and Amalekites slaughtered each other. Soon the huge, howling, horrified army was in full retreat back to the desert.

How did Gideon pull off this cool stunt? Gideon and his 300 commandos each had a trumpet and a jar with a torch burning in it. They were stationed on three sides

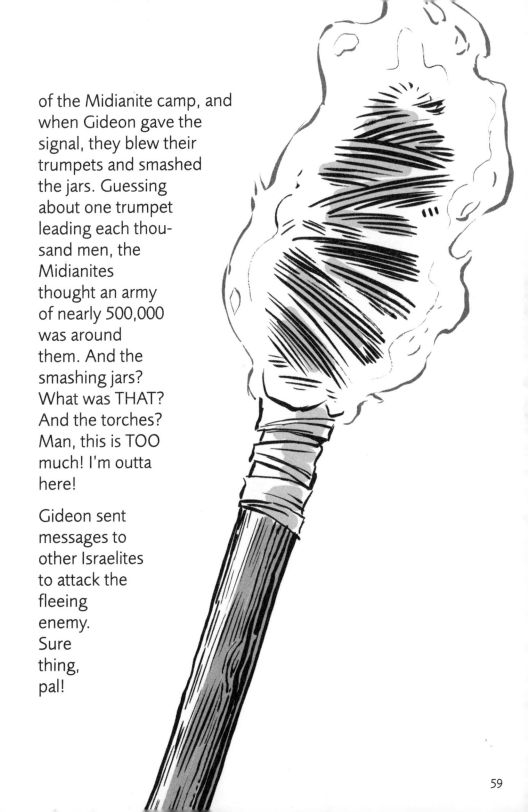

of the Midianite camp, and
when Gideon gave the
signal, they blew their
trumpets and smashed
the jars. Guessing
about one trumpet
leading each thou-
sand men, the
Midianites
thought an army
of nearly 500,000
was around
them. And the
smashing jars?
What was THAT?
And the torches?
Man, this is TOO
much! I'm outta
here!

Gideon sent
messages to
other Israelites
to attack the
fleeing
enemy.
Sure
thing,
pal!

The Israelites caught up with the retreating army along the Jordan River. All the enemy kings were killed, plus 120,000 of their soldiers. The rest of the army was scattered all over. Gideon and the Israelites probably laughed for years afterward how only 300 "commandos" with bags full of tricks and noise defeated an army of more than 135,000. Way to go, Gideon! Way to go, God!

GET SMARTER

The angel had called Gideon "mighty warrior." Gideon said, "Me? You must be mistaking me for someone else." Gideon didn't have a lot of confidence, because he thought the Lord had abandoned the Israelites. It took a lot to convince Gideon that the true God was talking to him. But God gave him a plan; Gideon trusted God, worked hard to prepare, and carried out that plan. When faced with a difficult job, you may think, "How can I get that done?" Well, any goal can start out looking difficult until you get up and start to work hard and do your best. Just make a start, trust God to help you, and you'll be on your way to the finish line.

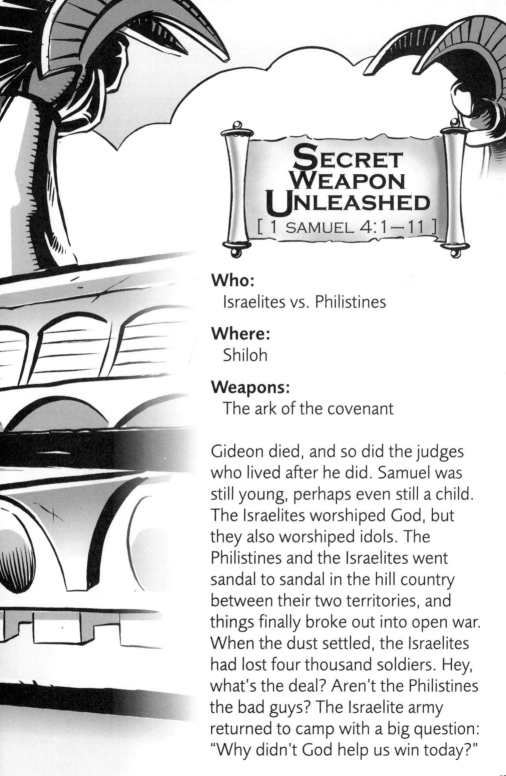

SECRET WEAPON UNLEASHED
[1 SAMUEL 4:1—11]

Who:
Israelites vs. Philistines

Where:
Shiloh

Weapons:
The ark of the covenant

Gideon died, and so did the judges who lived after he did. Samuel was still young, perhaps even still a child. The Israelites worshiped God, but they also worshiped idols. The Philistines and the Israelites went sandal to sandal in the hill country between their two territories, and things finally broke out into open war. When the dust settled, the Israelites had lost four thousand soldiers. Hey, what's the deal? Aren't the Philistines the bad guys? The Israelite army returned to camp with a big question: "Why didn't God help us win today?"

BATTLE MAP:
Secret Weapon

"Hey, wait minute!" they said. "The ark of the covenant! If we want God with us in battle, we gotta carry the ark with us. It worked for Joshua when he marched around Jericho, right? The priests carried the ark in front of the army and the walls of the city fell down. We take the ark with us and we're unbeatable! It's our secret weapon!"

This sounded like such a brilliant idea that the Israelites immediately lugged the ark down from the city of Shiloh to the battlefront. As soon as the ark arrived in camp the soldiers went crazy. The Philistines heard the shouts, and when they found out that the hubbub was about the ark, they moaned. "A god has come into the camp. We're in trouble! These are the

gods who struck the Egyptians with plagues." The Philistine generals stomped in, slapped some faces, and shouted, "Be strong, Philistines! Be men, and fight!"

The Israelites thought that since they had their secret weapon, the Philistines were toast. But the next day when the armies clashed, 30,000 Israelites were killed! Whoa! Bad news! And, worse news, the Philistines captured the ark! The Israelites had thought their unbeatable God would fight for them simply because they carried the ark into battle like a good luck charm. Wrong! God helped them when they obeyed him.

When they captured the ark, the Philistines decided Israel's God must not be very strong after all. They thought they had conquered him! Also wrong.

LEGEND

Battle Zone

Israelite Camp

Philistine Camp

Philistine Land

Path of the Ark

Strange things began to happen. When they gave the ark to their god, Dagon, by putting it in his temple, the stone idol of Dagon fell on its face in front of the ark and broke. Worse yet, everybody in any city the ark was in began getting sick, and many died.

None of the Philistine cities wanted the ark anywhere near them. After seven months, the Philistines got a plan together. They made gold statues as offerings to pay honor to Israel's God. They built a new cart, loaded the ark and the gold offerings, and hitched up two cows to haul it back to Israel. Finally, their mysterious troubles stopped.

What was in the ark?

The ark was a box—but what was in the box? Moses had placed in the ark the two stone tablets on which God had written the Ten Commandments, along with Aaron's staff that blossomed and bore nuts, and a pot of manna. That's all? Yes, that's all. What were you expecting rubies and diamonds and all kinds of gold loot? Hey! You've been watching too many movies! God's law is the greatest treasure!

GET COOLER

Do you have a secret weapon? The ark of the covenant was the symbol of God's presence with the Israelites. When the Israelites were serving God, he said, "I will go with you," and they knew their enemies would be defeated. If you believe in Jesus, God sends his Holy Spirit into your life and makes you his temple, the place where he lives. How cool is that! So wherever you go, it's better than carrying the ark with you. Every Christian has God's Holy Spirit. He is our secret weapon.

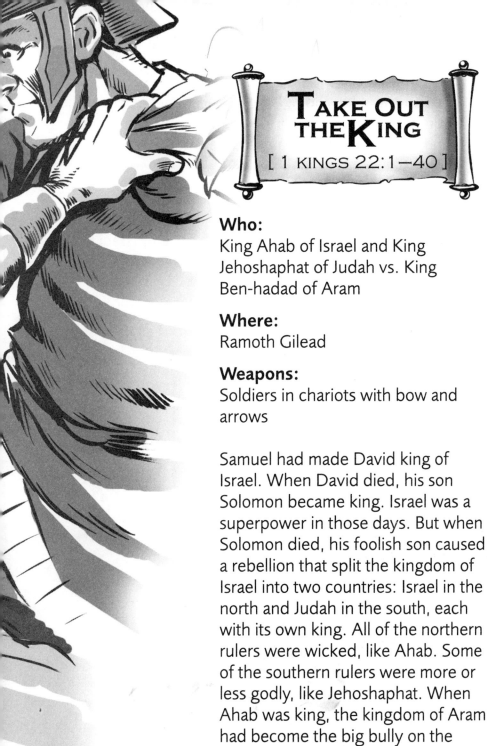

TAKE OUT THE KING

[1 KINGS 22:1–40]

Who:
King Ahab of Israel and King Jehoshaphat of Judah vs. King Ben-hadad of Aram

Where:
Ramoth Gilead

Weapons:
Soldiers in chariots with bow and arrows

Samuel had made David king of Israel. When David died, his son Solomon became king. Israel was a superpower in those days. But when Solomon died, his foolish son caused a rebellion that split the kingdom of Israel into two countries: Israel in the north and Judah in the south, each with its own king. All of the northern rulers were wicked, like Ahab. Some of the southern rulers were more or less godly, like Jehoshaphat. When Ahab was king, the kingdom of Aram had become the big bully on the block, and fought constant wars with the northern kingdom, Israel. The Arameans never did take over, but they kept trying and trying and trying, and sometimes they grabbed a few border cities.

BATTLE MAP:
Get the King!

King Ben-hadad of Aram and King Ahab of Israel had duked it out on several occasions. The Lord had helped Ahab stop Ben-hadad from invading Israel twice, but Ben-hadad still controlled the Israelite city of Ramoth Gilead. This bugged Ahab, and he talked to King Jehoshaphat of Judah about ganging up on Ben-hadad to get the city back. Now, Jehoshaphat was a godly guy, so he asked Ahab what God had told his prophets about this battle. Ahab assured him it was totally cool, but Jehoshaphat must have taken one look at Ahab's prophets and realized that they would say anything Ahab wanted to hear.

Jehoshaphat wanted the

Mediterranean
Sea

LAND OF THE
PHILISTINES

answer from a real prophet of the real God. OK, OK. Reluctantly, Ahab called on a guy named Micaiah — Mike, for short. Mike was always facing off with Ahab about the king's evil ways. Mike never had anything positive to say. This time he first mocked Ahab by saying what all the other prophets said. Then he said that God did want Ahab to go to war with Aram but that Ahab would die in the battle and the forces of Israel

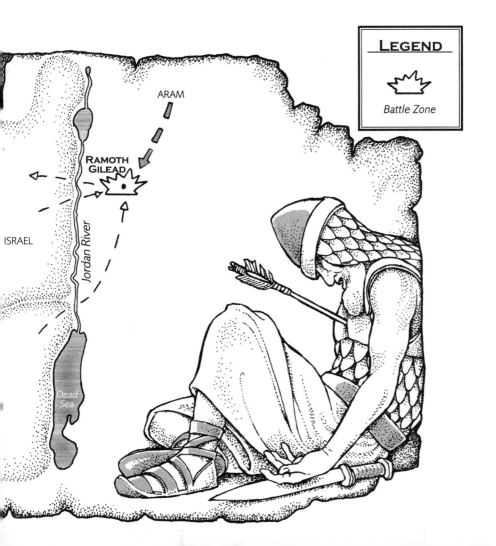

ARAM

RAMOTH
GILEAD

ISRAEL

Jordan River

Dead
Sea

LEGEND

Battle Zone

would be scattered. Hmmm—that's not good news. But Ahab and Jehoshaphat marched to Ramoth Gilead to face Ben-hadad's army anyway.

King Ben-hadad had a simple battle strategy: kill King Ahab. He figured that if Ahab were killed, the Israelite army would give up and scatter. Killing the enemy's king was a common tactic because it often worked. So Ben-hadad ordered his chariot commanders to seek out and destroy King Ahab.

Over in the Israelite camp, Ahab was a little nervous about what the prophet Mike had said. Ahab suggested that King Jehoshaphat wear his royal robes but that he, Ahab, would wear ordinary soldier clothes to blend in with the crowd and avoid being a target. The Arameans eventually figured out that the guy in the Armani suit wasn't Ahab. But during the fighting, an

Aramean archer shot randomly into the Israelite army, and THACK! the arrow flew into a crack in Ahab's body armor. Talk about a one-in-a-million shot. That evening, Ahab died from his wound, and his whole army ran from the battlefield. Ben-hadad not only kept control of Ramoth Gilead, but he killed King Ahab just as the Lord, through the prophet Mike (Micaiah), had said he would.

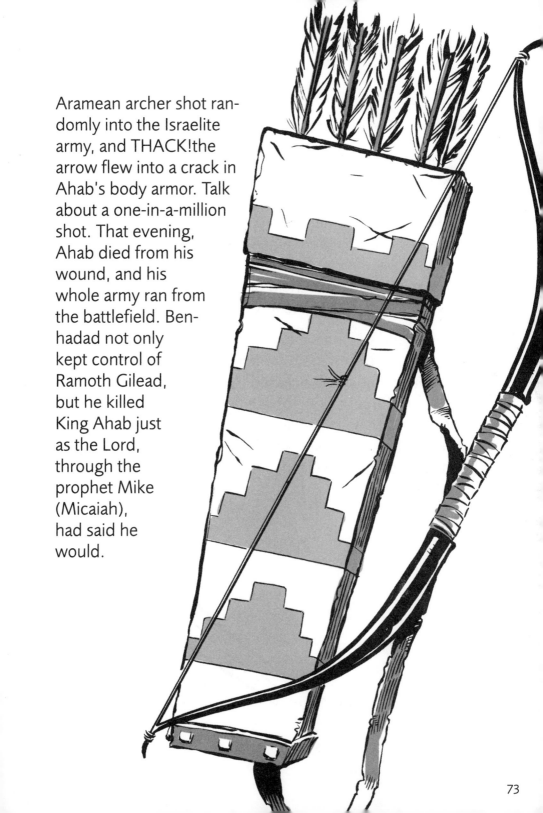

That's Gotta Hurt!

The ancient Egyptians had a whole lot of medical knowledge, everything from removing arrows to setting broken bones to crude brain surgery. It's likely that the Israelites brought a lot of that know-how with them when they came out of Egypt. But the average Israelite soldier had nobody but other soldiers to help doctor him up. (Careful when you yank out the arrow, Bud.)

Kings and generals may have traveled with their own doctors—perks of being the boss. A doctor's instruments would have included things like tourniquets, clamps, forceps (kind of like tweezers), arrow extractors, and scalpels (small knives). People used plants like opium to kill pain and things like wine, vinegar, and turpentine to clean wounds. (Ooh! Hurts just to think about it!)

GET SMARTER

War was a nasty business and was a source of huge stress for the kings and queens of the ancient world. To fight or not to fight? Would the outcome be victory or slavery? It was only natural for rulers to seek out seers or prophets to try to discover if God was on their side. God often used wartime to demonstrate his love, power, and protection or, in some cases, to teach a hard lesson. He often used prophets to talk to the rulers of the ancient world, but sometimes the rulers just didn't listen. When you get advice from godly people in your life, like your parents or pastor, pay attention and think about the things that they tell you.

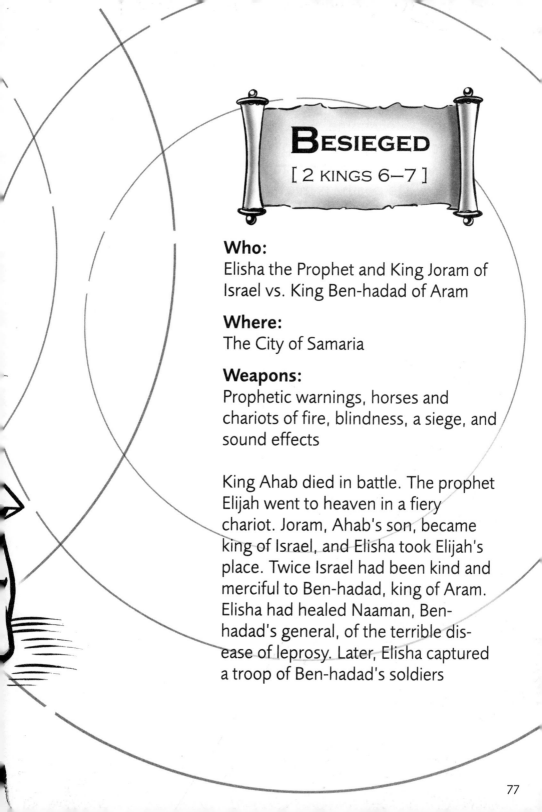

Besieged
[2 Kings 6–7]

Who:
Elisha the Prophet and King Joram of Israel vs. King Ben-hadad of Aram

Where:
The City of Samaria

Weapons:
Prophetic warnings, horses and chariots of fire, blindness, a siege, and sound effects

King Ahab died in battle. The prophet Elijah went to heaven in a fiery chariot. Joram, Ahab's son, became king of Israel, and Elisha took Elijah's place. Twice Israel had been kind and merciful to Ben-hadad, king of Aram. Elisha had healed Naaman, Ben-hadad's general, of the terrible disease of leprosy. Later, Elisha captured a troop of Ben-hadad's soldiers and chariots, then gave them a great feast, and sent them safely home. So why was Ben-hadad's army back at Samaria, the capital of Israel, besieging the city and starving all its people to death? Is this how he says "thank you" for the good things Elisha did for him?

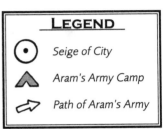

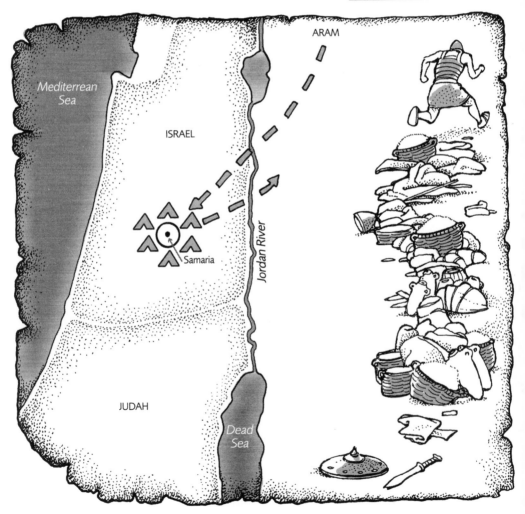

BATTLE MAP:
Samarian Siege

This siege was a long one, and finally there was so little food left in the city that people were paying big bucks for donkey heads and shells off seeds—in other words, garbage. In some Bibles, the word "seedpods" is translated "dove's dung." Gross! Even more horrible, people had begun killing and eating their babies. You get the picture—the people were VERY hungry.

King Joram blamed God and God's prophet, Elisha, for the mess they were in. But Elisha told Joram that by the next day, there would be mountains of food in Samaria, and it would be selling at bargain prices. The king's right hand man scoffed. "No way!" Elisha replied, "But you will not eat any of it." Doubters don't get to dig in, you see.

Four men with leprosy were sitting just outside the city gates. As the sun was going down, they decided to go out and surrender to the Aramean army, since they were starving to death anyway. They walked into

the camp without meeting a single guard. Hello? They looked around – but the place was completely abandoned. It creeped them out! Why would the soldiers leave their tents, belongings, and food, and even their horses and donkeys still tied up? God had turned up the volume on his surround-sound special effects, and the Arameans thought they heard chariots and horses and a great army. The entire camp emptied out! But the Arameans were the only ones who heard the noise.

What a find for the starving men! Mountains of food, enough for an entire army – or a starving city! They hurried back and, with mouths full of food, spread the news. King Joram thought this was too good to be true. Yeah, it had to be a trap to lure the Israelites out and then ambush them. Joram sent two chariots to scout out the situation. The chariots followed the trail of thrown-away clothing and equipment all the way to the Jordan River. The siege was over.

The Samaritans threw open the gates and swarmed out! They stripped the enemy camp of everything. And just as Elisha had said, there was cheap food for everybody. Oh. And remember the king's deputy? He got knocked down and trampled to death by the rush of starving people squeezing through the gates.

Hired Help

When Ben-hadad heard the noise of a huge army, he was sure that the Israelites had hired the armies of Egypt and the Hittites to fight for them. Rulers in

those days often rented their armies to other kingdoms. Weaker kingdoms in trouble often shelled out a lot of gold to stronger countries to get them to come to the rescue.

Using mercenaries is another way to get help. Mervenaries are independent bands of professional soldiers, who don't belong to any country's army. They will fight for whomever pays their wages.

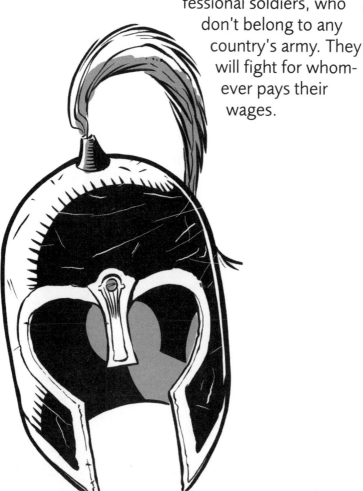

GET DEEPER

A situation may seem impossible to us, but it never is to God. He can always turn it around. During the siege of Samaria, the Israelites went from having nothing to eat to having way more than enough in one day. God said, "I am the Lord . Is anything too hard for me?" (Jeremiah 32:26) With God, ALL things are possible, so feel free to talk to God about any impossible situations you get into. Remember, God is on the job, he cares, and he is strong enough to deal with anything that happens to you.

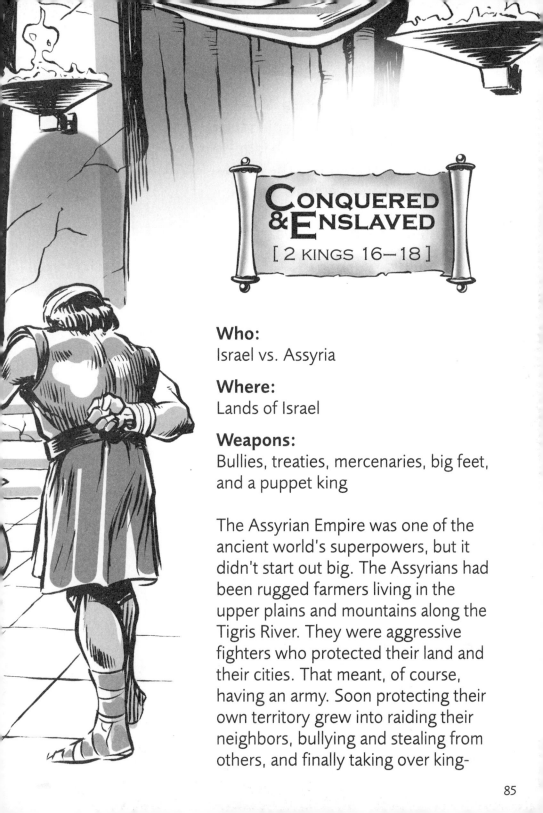

CONQUERED & ENSLAVED

[2 KINGS 16–18]

Who:
Israel vs. Assyria

Where:
Lands of Israel

Weapons:
Bullies, treaties, mercenaries, big feet, and a puppet king

The Assyrian Empire was one of the ancient world's superpowers, but it didn't start out big. The Assyrians had been rugged farmers living in the upper plains and mountains along the Tigris River. They were aggressive fighters who protected their land and their cities. That meant, of course, having an army. Soon protecting their own territory grew into raiding their neighbors, bullying and stealing from others, and finally taking over kingdoms all over the place. They built great cities and settled their own people into the rich farmlands they captured. They grew into the largest empire that the ancient world had ever seen. It lasted three hundred years.

BATTLE MAP:
Enter the Assyrians

Here's how the Assyrians ended up in Israel's part of the world: Judah had a bad king named Ahaz, and one day the king of Aram and the king of Israel decided they'd gang up on Ahaz. They were soon besieging Jerusalem, the capital city of Judah. King Ahaz was in a reallllly tight situation. He raided his palace piggy bank, stripped off all the gold and silver from God's temple, and paid King Tiglath-Pileser, king of Assyria, to save

KING OF ARAM

KING OF ISRAEL

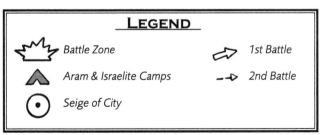

LEGEND

⚡ Battle Zone

🔺 Aram & Israelite Camps

⊙ Seige of City

⇨ 1st Battle

⇢ 2nd Battle

ASSYRIA

DAMASCUS

ARAM

Assyrian Army Captures Israel

ISRAEL

Samaria

Jordan River

Mediterranean Sea

LAND OF THE PHILISTINES

Jerusalem

Dead
Sea

JUDAH

Judah from Israel and Aram.

Assyria was the biggest empire around, so hiring them was like getting the Terminator on your side.

Tiglath-Pileser liked the gold so much that he gathered his tough Assyrian soldiers, attacked Aram, and captured the Aramean capital, Damascus. He killed the king of Aram and sent the people of Damascus up north as slaves. Take that, Aram! Lesson learned: There's always a bigger bully around the corner. Uh— speaking of that bully around the corner—he's now Judah and Israel's new next-door neighbor and is breathing down everyone's neck.

God warned Israel and Judah over and over through his prophets, No more idol worship, no more evil! Period! They didn't listen, and judgment day was coming. First, Assyria invaded Israel and carried many Israelites to distant lands as slaves. An Israelite named Hoshea promised to pay tribute to Assyria, so the Assyrians made him the new king of Israel. Long live puppet-king Hoshea! In time, the Assyrian Empire also got a new king, Shalmaneser.

As long as Hoshea and the Israelites paid Shalmaneser gifts year after year after year, the Assyrians left them alone. These "gifts," called tribute, were nothing more than protection money, which meant, "As long as you pay us, we'll 'protect' you from us and let you live." The Israelites paid tribute for twelve years. Then King

Hoshea got tired of it and stopped paying tribute. That didn't go over well with Shalmaneser.

Shalmaneser attacked Israel's capital city, Samaria, and

set siege against it for three years! Can you imagine being stuck inside a city for three years? The streets were full of starving, dying people. It was a nightmare.

Samaria finally caved, and Shalmaneser entered. Then he attacked the whole land of Israel and sent everyone away as slaves. The kingdom of Israel was no more. It was completely gone. The kingdom of Judah was hanging on by kissing big Assyrian feet.

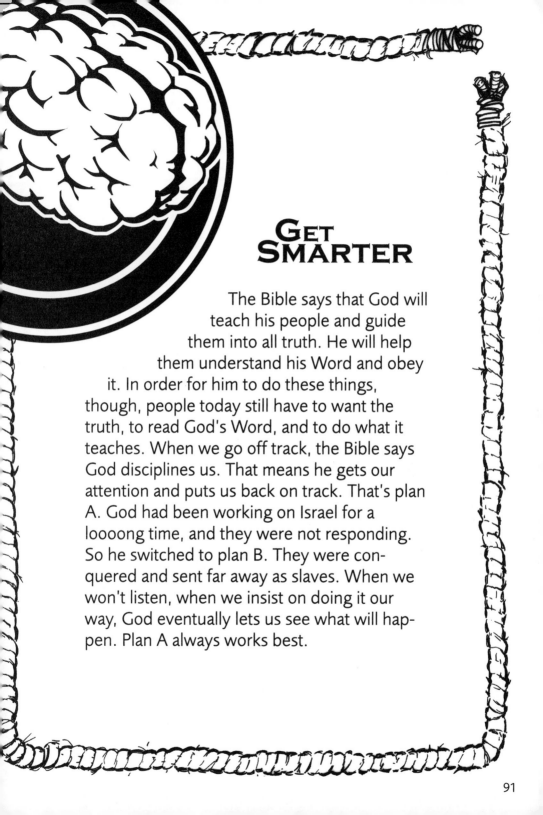

GET SMARTER

The Bible says that God will teach his people and guide them into all truth. He will help them understand his Word and obey it. In order for him to do these things, though, people today still have to want the truth, to read God's Word, and to do what it teaches. When we go off track, the Bible says God disciplines us. That means he gets our attention and puts us back on track. That's plan A. God had been working on Israel for a loooong time, and they were not responding. So he switched to plan B. They were conquered and sent far away as slaves. When we won't listen, when we insist on doing it our way, God eventually lets us see what will happen. Plan A always works best.

THE BATTLE ANGEL

[2 KINGS 12:13—19:37]

Who:
The Prophet Isaiah and King Hezekiah of Judah vs. King Sennacherib of Assyria

Where:
Jerusalem

Weapons:
Siege, prophecy, prayer, and an angel warrior

If you start paying bullies protection money to leave you alone, they don't ever want you to stop paying them. Hezekiah had been king of Judah for fourteen years when he found that out. Hezekiah was a good king and wanted to rule Judah God's way. He not only smashed the idols in his kingdom, but he also stopped paying tribute to Shalmaneser, king of Assyria. He got away with this for several years because Shalmaneser was busy conquering Israel. Besides, Hezekiah had a strong army.

LEGEND

Assyrian Camps

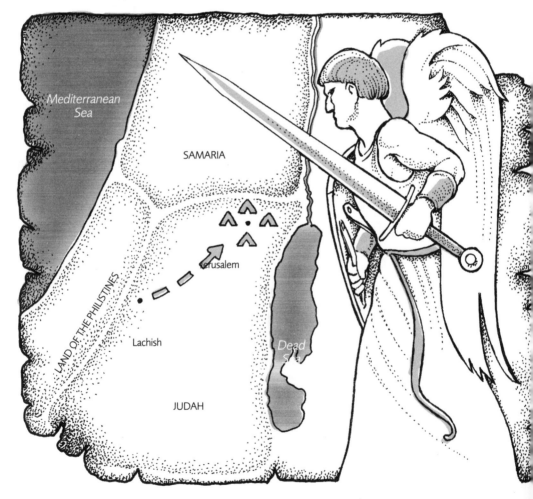

BATTLE MAP:
Help from Heaven

A new tough guy named Sennacherib became king of Assyria. Sennacherib marched south, determined to conquer Judah. He had conquered all the fortified citiesof Judah, when Hezekiah chickened out and tried to pay him off. Independence? Who us? Just joking! Hezekiah sent Sennacherib 11 tons of silver and a ton of gold. But Sennacherib kept coming anyway. His army surrounded Jerusalem and prepared for a long siege.

Hezekiah sent his top aides out to talk to the Assyrian field commander. The commander ordered them to surrender Jerusalem. If Hezekiah refused, the entire city would suffer a long and agonizing death. After all, the commander reasoned, what hope did the people of Jerusalem have? None of the gods worshiped in other cities had been able to save *them* from the Assyrians, so the God worshiped in Jerusalem couldn't save that city either. It was their choice: life as slaves far away or death inside the city. No doubt about it, King Hezekiah was in a fix.

A little later, Sennacherib sent a threatening note to Hezekiah and it went something like this...

Dear Hezekiah:

You're toast! Nothing can save you from me! And don't think your Hebrew god can save you! No way. Unless you surrender now, I'm going to pound you into dust. So get with the program and surrender. Have a nice day.

Yours Truly,
King Sennacherib

Hezekiah knew that he needed God's help. He did a very wise thing. He took Sennacherib's letter the one that mocked God into the temple, spread it out for God to read, and prayed. God read it. Oh, yeah. Isaiah sent a message to Hezekiah, "Sennacherib will not enter this city—ever." That night the angel of the Lord killed 185,000 soldiers in the Assyrian camp. Talk about wiping out the enemy! When Hezekiah woke up the next day and saw the Assyrian body count he knew how powerful God was. You would think Sennacherib would have known too. He quietly ordered his remaining troops home. But the huge thing God had done didn't change Sennacherib's arrogant mind. He never came back to Jerusalem, though, because two of his sons killed him while he was in church with his idol god.

Army Parts

The Assyrian army was a well-organized fighting machine with many different parts. The king had his personal bodyguards, usually an army of several thousand. The regular army was a larger body of soldiers made up of Assyrians and also soldiers drafted from defeated armies. The special forces such as archers, cavalry, and charioteers were usually made up of loyal Assyrians. The quartermaster corps traveled with the army and supplied food and fresh water to the troops. The corps of engineers built the roads and bridges for the army. And what army would be complete without army intelligence, the small but elite corps of spies and scouts who found out information about the enemy?

But a fat lot of good even 185,000 soldiers would do the king if GOD got mad at him!

GET SMARTER

When you're in a jam, what's the first thing you do? Hezekiah tried everything to make Assyria go away and forget about him. When all else failed, he went to God for help. God showed his great power by destroying the Assyrians. When we pray, God doesn't always get us out of trouble. But remember, even when you are in trouble, God is right there in it with you. Ask him to help you. If he doesn't save you out of the trouble, ask him to give you courage and strength to go through it.

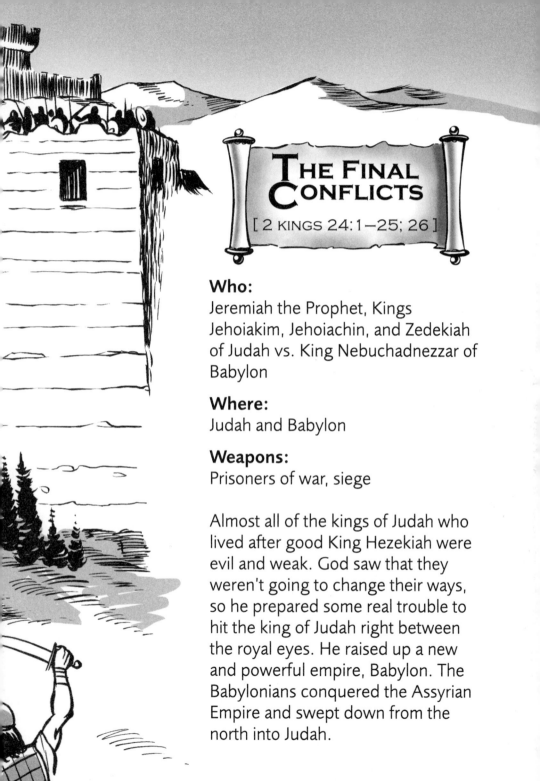

THE FINAL CONFLICTS

[2 KINGS 24:1–25; 26]

Who:
Jeremiah the Prophet, Kings
Jehoiakim, Jehoiachin, and Zedekiah
of Judah vs. King Nebuchadnezzar of
Babylon

Where:
Judah and Babylon

Weapons:
Prisoners of war, siege

Almost all of the kings of Judah who
lived after good King Hezekiah were
evil and weak. God saw that they
weren't going to change their ways,
so he prepared some real trouble to
hit the king of Judah right between
the royal eyes. He raised up a new
and powerful empire, Babylon. The
Babylonians conquered the Assyrian
Empire and swept down from the
north into Judah.

BATTLE MAP:
Final Conflicts

The prophet Jeremiah warned the kings of Judah that it was no use for them to ask for God's help against Nebuchadnezzar, king of Babylon. God was fed up with his people's disobedience and sin. King Neb marched into little Judah and took over, and for three years King Jehoiakim paid tribute. Then he decided, Enough! I'm keeping the tribute money myself! (So what if Jeremiah says I'll be buried like a donkey!) Surprise, surprise! Neb came back, attacked Jerusalem again, and took Jehoiakim to prison in Babylon.

Jehoiakim's evil and stubborn son Jehoiachin became king. He decided, Duh, I think I'll rebel against Babylon. He lasted only three months and ten days, which has to be a record of some kind. Nebuchadnezzar came and attacked Jerusalem again! Jehoiachin and all his officials quickly surrendered. They were shipped off to Babylon too. King Neb rounded up more than eight thousand of Jerusalem's most important citizens and marched them away as slaves. (It was during one of these three attacks that Nebuchadnezzar took Daniel and his friends to Babylon as captives.)

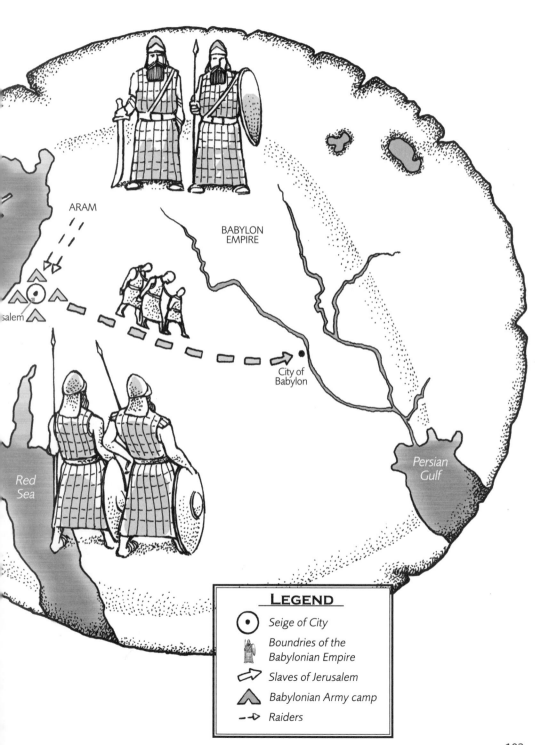

ARAM

BABYLON
EMPIRE

salem

City of
Babylon

Red
Sea

Persian
Gulf

LEGEND

Seige of City

Boundries of the
Babylonian Empire

Slaves of Jerusalem

Babylonian Army camp

Raiders

Nebuchadnezzar left Jehoiachin's uncle, Zedekiah, to rule over Judah. Now, had Zedekiah learned from what happened to his brother and his nephew? Nope. He disobeyed God too, and after nine years he also refused to obey Nebuchadnezzar. Was this guy stupid or what? Neb stormed back to Jerusalem and set siege to it again. Jeremiah told Zedekiah that God was against Jerusalem. People could stay in the city and die, or they could save their lives by surrendering to the Babylonians. After two years, the city was starving to death. Then Neb crashed through the wall of the city, but Zedekiah and his army slipped out during the night. They left the starving citizens of Jerusalem to face the Babylonians alone. Nice guys.

The Babylonians caught up with Zedekiah near Jericho. Then they took everything of value from Jerusalem and torched the city. Even God's beautiful temple, that Solomon had built, was completely destroyed. The great kingdom God had given his people in Canaan was gone.

The Babylonians controlled a huge boomerang-shaped section of land that included the Tigris and Euphrates Rivers and the Mediterranean coast all the way down to Egypt. Before Nebuchadnezzar was king of Babylon, he commanded the kingdom's army and defeated the powerful Egyptians. Soon he took over one kingdom after another.

His capital city, Babylon, was one of the most impressive cities of the ancient world. As many as 200,000 people lived there. The city was surrounded by outer walls, defensive towers, and moats. It had eight huge bronze gates and a brick wall 21 feet thick and 59 feet tall. The city even had a number of large moats. One of the city's moats was 150 feet wide—that's half a football field.

GET SMARTER

God used the Israelites when they first came into Canaan as a judgment force to drive out and kill the extremely wicked people who lived there. Fast forward many years and the Israelites have become as wicked as the people they had killed. They won't obey God, but they still think they'll be OK, because they're Israelites, "God's people." So God raised up a judgment army against them—the Assyrians—then Nebuchadnezzar and the Babylonians and took them out of the promised land. If you know the truth about Jesus and you've become a Christian, that doesn't give you a license to do whatever you want—to sin. Ask God to help you to be a Christian, not just someone who knows what a Christian believes.

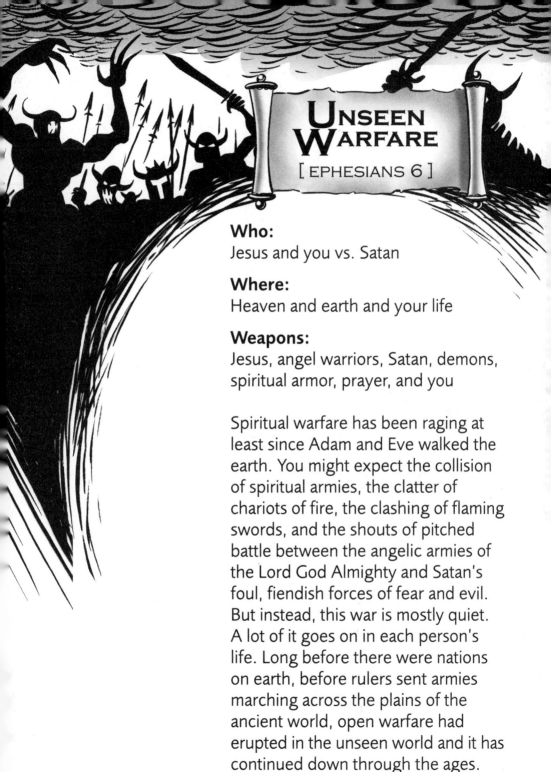

UNSEEN WARFARE

[EPHESIANS 6]

Who:
Jesus and you vs. Satan

Where:
Heaven and earth and your life

Weapons:
Jesus, angel warriors, Satan, demons, spiritual armor, prayer, and you

Spiritual warfare has been raging at least since Adam and Eve walked the earth. You might expect the collision of spiritual armies, the clatter of chariots of fire, the clashing of flaming swords, and the shouts of pitched battle between the angelic armies of the Lord God Almighty and Satan's foul, fiendish forces of fear and evil. But instead, this war is mostly quiet. A lot of it goes on in each person's life. Long before there were nations on earth, before rulers sent armies marching across the plains of the ancient world, open warfare had erupted in the unseen world and it has continued down through the ages.

BATTLE MAP: A New Battle Zone

When the angel Gabriel brought a message to the prophet Daniel, he told Daniel he'd been trying to hack his way through enemy lines for 21 days, but the demon prince of Persia had resisted him. Gabriel finally broke through when the warrior angel, Michael, came to help him fight. (See Daniel 10:12–13.) Hundreds of years later, Satan stopped the apostle Paul from going to the city of Thessalonica. (See 1 Thessalonians 2:18.) And the battles continue to this day!

The most important battles don't involve pyrotechnics, tanks, or missiles. They are not the ones we see on TV or learn about in history books, but they are the unseen wars of the spirit world, where the forces of God and of the Devil are involved in a life and death struggle fighting for people's souls. It's a battleground out there–uh–in there! There's a battle in us and a battle outside of us. The Bible says, "Our struggle is not against flesh and blood, but against the rulers, against the authorities, against the powers of this dark world and against the spiritual forces of evil in the heavenly realms" (Ephesians 6:12).

Jesus told us what each force—light and darkness—is trying to do: "The thief comes only to steal and kill and destroy; I have come that they may have life, and have it to the full" (John 10:10). The thief, Satan, tries to stop people from knowing Christ and believing in him. He also tries to stop Christians from spreading the news about Jesus.

When Christians make a habit of sinning, they are fighting on the enemy's side instead of fighting for Christ.

The Bible says, "Do not give the devil a foothold" (Ephesians 4:27). That means, when we sin, we give Satan a small base of operations, and he uses that to try to get us to sin more. He likes to keep dragging us further and further his way, bit by bit, until we're not following God any more. All Christians are growing, and we all sin. If we

ask God to forgive us and to help us, he will.

Satan blinds unbelievers to the truth that God loves people and sent Jesus to save them. Those who know the truth must therefore fight by their prayers and by their words and their lives to rescue people into the kingdom of God's Son (Colossians 1:13) by telling them

God's truth. In the Old Testament, God used the Israelites as his army on earth. Now Christians are God's army, and our new weapon is the good news about Jesus Christ dying for our sin so we don't have to. The enemy is no longer big, tough Canaanites or Assyrians, or even a terrorist like Osama. Our enemies are the devil and sin—enemies we can't see but that are just as real. This new battleground is all over the world and in our own selves. We "fight the good fight of faith" (1 Timothy 6:12).

GET DEEPER
Armed for Battle

Satan lost the war when Jesus died on the cross. But he will keep on fighting—until Jesus comes back and destroys him completely. Our enemy still has his army of demons, and he's still around causing problems for God's people. God gives us spiritual armor to protect ourselves. So let's get suited up.

The Belt of Truth:
Soldiers wore belts to keep their armor together and to hang their swords on. Wearing the belt of truth means you tell the truth—always. When we know God's truth, the Bible, we won't get confused about what is real or what is lies.

Breastplate of Righteousness:
A breastplate was the old-time version of a bulletproof

vest. When you wear the breastplate of righteous-
ness, it means you protect your heart from sin.
Jesus died for us and our sins are forgiven. We are
righteous only because of what he did. We need to
keep our breastplate in place, and we do that by
doing things God's way, and also by quickly asking
God to forgive us and help us when we blow it.

Shoes of Readiness:
Soldiers aren't ready for battle if they are barefooted.
God wants his soldiers to be ready to tell others the
good news that Jesus died so their sins can be forgiven.

Shield of Faith:
A shield protected a soldier from enemy arrows. If you
trust God, even when you don't understand why bad
things happen, you are holding up faith like a shield.
Faith means believing in God and always trusting in his
love. That's important because Satan loves to whisper
doubt in our ear.

When we choose to believe God, and not Satan's lies,
the shield of faith works to block those fiery arrows of
doubt the devil shoots at us.

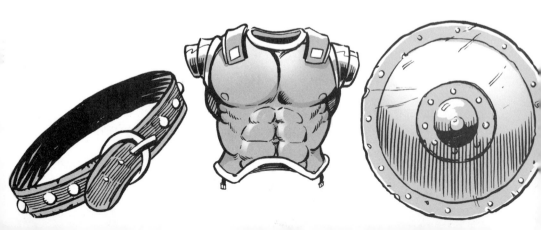

Helmet of Salvation:

Soldiers wore helmets to protect their heads. A helmet protects our brain and a spiritual helmet protects our souls. Salvation protects us forever!

Salvation is Jesus delivering us from sin and Satan's power. He does this when we ask him to forgive us for our sins and give us eternal life.

Sword of the Spirit:

God's Word is the Holy Spirit's sword. A sword is both an offensive and a defensive weapon, meaning we can use our sword both to defend ourselves from Satan's negativity and to attack his lies, by spreading the truth. God's word has a razor-sharp edge. (See Hebrews 4:12.) The Bible is the tool the Holy Spirit uses to show us the truth about God and about ourselves. (See Hebrews 4:12.) The apostle Paul tells us to wear our whole armor every day, to always stay on red alert, and to always pray for each other.

ARMAGEDDON

[REVELATION 14:17–20;
16:12–16; 19:11–21]

Who:
Jesus and the Armies of Heaven vs. the Dragon, the Beast, and the False Prophet and their Army

Where:
Armageddon

Weapons:
Earthly and flying warhorses, human and angel armies with swords

Ever heard people talk about the Battle of Armageddon? It's a battle described in the book of Revelation. It truly will be earth's final conflict, the biggest, bloodiest battle ever fought between good and evil on planet earth! There has never been a battle like it before and (fortunately) there will never be one like it again.

Battle Map:
The Last Battle

Revelation contains lots of visions and symbolic stuff. For example, when it talks about a great red, seven-headed dragon in Revelation 12, it's not talking about an actual dragon it's talking about the devil, Satan. Because Revelation is so mysterious, Christians have many different ideas about what its visions mean. Some feel that the entire book is symbolic, that even the battles it talks about are not real battles. Other Christians believe that every battle and every plague will happen just the way Revelation describes and soon! They think that a wicked person–a Devil-possessed dictator called the Antichrist–will become ruler over the entire world and insist that everyone worship him. Then he gets wind that Jesus is returning to earth, so he gathers an army of 200 million and marches to Israel to do battle with Jesus in the Valley of Jezreel. This wicked ruler sets up a command post at Armageddon and waits.

Suddenly, the heavens split open and Jesus comes "riding down on a great white warhorse, leading the huge armies of heaven, also on riding white horses. Jesus lands on the Mount of Olives, the mountain splits in two in a great earthquake, and a valley opens up all the way from Jerusalem to the Valley of Jezreel. The Antichrist's armies foolishly open fire on the

Legend

⟳ Path of Christ's Army

⌂ Anti-christ's Command post

▲ Anti-christ's Headquarters

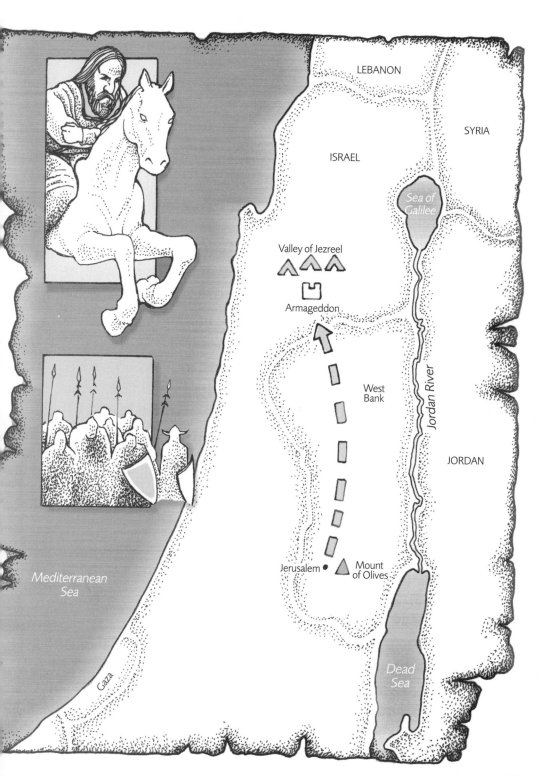

LEBANON

SYRIA

ISRAEL

Sea of
Galilee

Valley of Jezreel

Armageddon

West
Bank

Jordan River

JORDAN

Jerusalem • △ Mount
of Olives

Mediterranean
Sea

Gaza

Dead
Sea

flying cavalry, but they are no match, and Jesus' supernatural army sweeps down and begins slaughtering the Antichrist's army by the millions. When the Battle of Armageddon is over, Jesus Christ begins to reign and rule in person over the earth.

What happens when Jesus returns and sets up his kingdom on earth? Well, there are different opinions about the exact timing of different events, but the fact is, we really do know a lot of amazing details about what Jesus' kingdom will be like. Revelation 21:2–4 tells us that there will be no more death, mourning, crying, or pain—that definitely means no more battles! Just heaven forever!

The following verses tell about the kingdom of God that is coming and they give a very amazing picture of the future.

"Behold, I will create new heavens and a new earth. The wolf and the lamb shall feed together, and the lion will eat straw like the ox...They will neither harm nor destroy on all my holy mountain" (Isaiah 65:17, 25).

"They will beat their swords into plowshares and their spears into pruning hooks. Nation will not take up sword against nation, nor will they train for war anymore" (Isaiah 2:4).

No more war ever again! Finally!

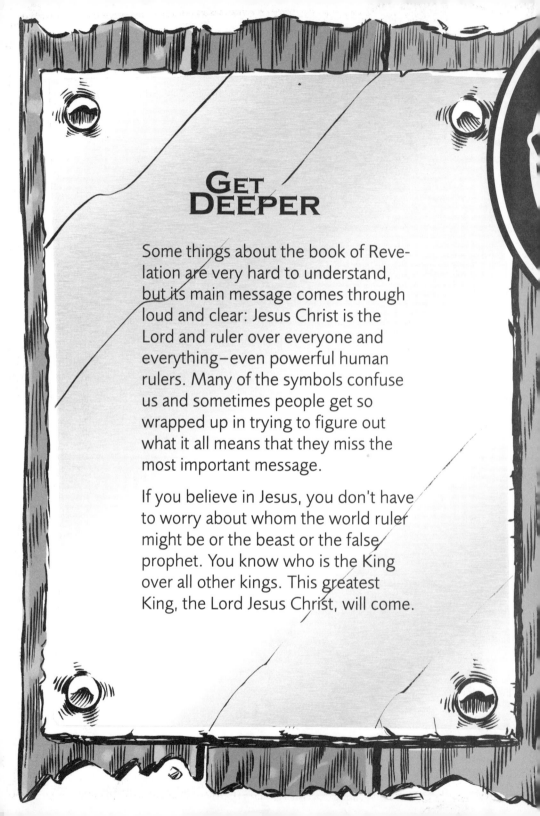

GET DEEPER

Some things about the book of Revelation are very hard to understand, but its main message comes through loud and clear: Jesus Christ is the Lord and ruler over everyone and everything—even powerful human rulers. Many of the symbols confuse us and sometimes people get so wrapped up in trying to figure out what it all means that they miss the most important message.

If you believe in Jesus, you don't have to worry about whom the world ruler might be or the beast or the false prophet. You know who is the King over all other kings. This greatest King, the Lord Jesus Christ, will come.

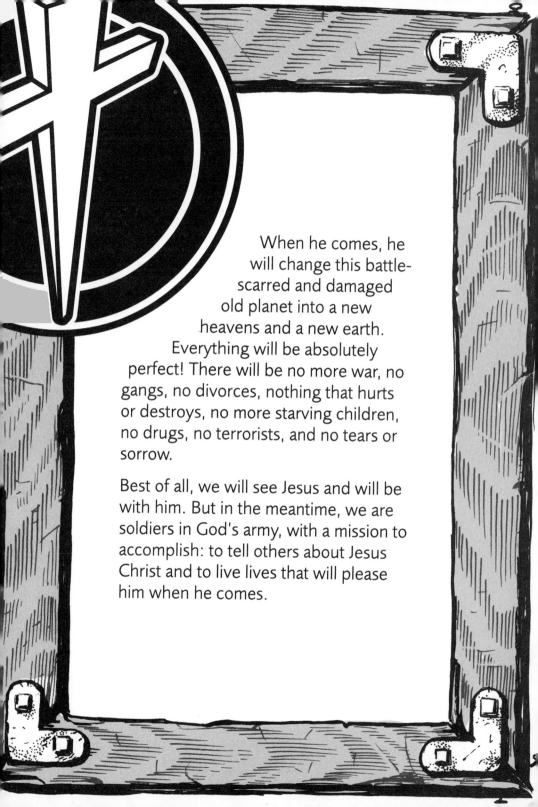

When he comes, he will change this battle-scarred and damaged old planet into a new heavens and a new earth. Everything will be absolutely perfect! There will be no more war, no gangs, no divorces, nothing that hurts or destroys, no more starving children, no drugs, no terrorists, and no tears or sorrow.

Best of all, we will see Jesus and will be with him. But in the meantime, we are soldiers in God's army, with a mission to accomplish: to tell others about Jesus Christ and to live lives that will please him when he comes.

2:52 Soul Gear™ Laptop fiction books–
Technological thrillers that will keep you on the edge of your seat...

Laptop 1: Reality Shift
They Changed the Future
Written by Christopher P. N. Maselli
Softcover 0-310-70338-7

Laptop 2: Double–Take
Things are Not What They Seem
Written by Christopher P. N. Maselli
Softcover 0-310-70339-5

Available now at your local bookstore!

More suspense & intrigue coming spring 2003

Laptop 3: Explosive Secrets
*Not Everything Lost
is Meant to be Found*
Written by Christopher P. N. Maselli
Softcover 0-310-70340-9

Laptop 4: Power Play
Beware of Broken Promises
Written by Christopher P. N. Maselli
Softcover 0-310-70341-7

Zonder**kidz**™

The 2:52 Boys Bible–
the "ultimate *manual*" for boys!

The 2:52 Boys Bible, NIV
General Editor Rick Osborne

From the metal-looking cover to the cool features inside, *The 2:52 Boys Bible, NIV* is filled with tons of fun and interesting facts –yup, even gross ones, too!–that only a boy could appreciate. Based on Luke 2:52: "And Jesus grew in wisdom and stature, and in favor with God and men," this Bible will help boys ages 8-12 become more like Jesus mentally, physically, spiritually, and socially–Smarter, Stronger, Deeper, and Cooler!

Hardcover 0-310-70320-4
Softcover 0-310-70552-5

Zonder**kidz**™

Introducing a fun, new CD holder for young boys that has a rubber 2:52 Soul Gear™ logo patch stitched onto cool nylon material. This cover will look great with the newly released 2:52 Soul Gear™ products. The interior has 12 sleeves to hold 24 favorite CDs.

$9.99 ($15.50 Cdn)

ISBN: 0-310-99033-5
UPC: 025986990336

Introducing a fun, new book and Bible Cover for young boys that will look great with the newly released 2:52 Soul Gear™ products. It features a rubber 2:52 logo patch stitched down onto nylon material. The zipper pull is black with 2:52 embroidered in gray. The interior has pen/pencil holders.

$14.99 ($22.50 Cdn) each

Large	ISBN: 0-310-98824-1
	UPC: 025986988241
Med	ISBN: 0-310-98823-3
	UPC: 025986988234

inspirio
The gift group of Zondervan

We want to hear from you. Please send your comments
about this book to us in care of the address below.
Thank you.

Zonder**kidz**™

Grand Rapids, MI 49530
www.zonderkidz.com